History and genealogy of the Byrd family, from the early part of 1700 A. D., when they first settled at Muddy Creek, Accomack County, Virginia, down to A. D. 1907 - Primary Source Edition

Byrd, Colwell Patterson, 1829-

Nabu Public Domain Reprints:

You are holding a reproduction of an original work published before 1923 that is in the public domain in the United States of America, and possibly other countries. You may freely copy and distribute this work as no entity (individual or corporate) has a copyright on the body of the work. This book may contain prior copyright references, and library stamps (as most of these works were scanned from library copies). These have been scanned and retained as part of the historical artifact.

This book may have occasional imperfections such as missing or blurred pages, poor pictures, errant marks, etc. that were either part of the original artifact, or were introduced by the scanning process. We believe this work is culturally important, and despite the imperfections, have elected to bring it back into print as part of our continuing commitment to the preservation of printed works worldwide. We appreciate your understanding of the imperfections in the preservation process, and hope you enjoy this valuable book.

HISTORY AND GENEALOGY

OF THE

BYRD FAMILY

From the early part of 1700 A. D., when they first settled at Muddy Creek, Accomack County, Virginia, down to A. D. 1907

BY

COLWELL P. BYRD

OF POCOMOKE CITY

MARYLAND

1908

CS
71
.B9993
1908

Byrd, Colwell Patterson, 1829–
  History and genealogy of the Byrd family, from the early part of 1700 A. D., when they first settled at Muddy Creek, Accomack County, Virginia, down to A. D. 1907. Pocomoke City, Md., 1908.
  125 p. illus. 19 cm.

53666

1. Byrd family.

CS71.B9993   1908

Library of Congress

58-53684

1909839

COLWELL P. BYRD, AGED 79 YEARS
POCOMOKE CITY, MD.

Copyrighted 1908
By F. W. Byrd.

This brief volume which has been a pleasurable calling to the writer, is dedicated to his devoted grand-daughters

ELIZABETH GRACE OLDHAM
HALLIE JOHNSON BYRD
ELIZABETH FRANKLIN BYRD

as a token of appreciation of the tender and gentle affection manifested toward me.

COLWELL P. BYRD.

PREFACE

THIS little book, containing a brief sketch of the buried history of this worthy family, it is hoped will be a source of gratification to many who may read it, and produce a desire in them to know more of those from whom they are descended.

What first prompted me to take some pains to learn long-forgotten facts about the Byrd family was the desire of some of the younger members to know something of their ancestors, and finding them worthy, it is to be hoped that they will strive to imitate their deeds and emulate their virtues.

INTRODUCTION

THE author of this work has a vivid appreciation of the difficulties of his task. Without special study of similar efforts, without knowledge of heraldry, with but limited scholastic acquirements, with the best years of his manhood given to the arduous labor of a brickmason, notwithstanding his ripe age of seventy-eight years, he has nevertheless attempted to unravel the tangled skein of a family history dating back traditionally to the time of the first settlement of the Byrd family on Muddy Creek, Accomack county, Virginia, early in the eighteenth century. Perhaps, had he known at the beginning all the obstacles he was destined afterwards to meet, he would have been deterred from the undertaking; but he set himself to

the task, and the difficulties which he encountered seemed to him, as they arose, so many added reasons why he should press the work to a successful issue.

That he has succeeded in a perfect history he is far from thinking; indeed, he is painfully aware of its imperfections, more aware, probably, than any one can be who has not tried to do a similar work. Nevertheless it is his desire that this brief history will be a source of great gratification to many who may read it, and will be found satisfactory, to some extent, to those who are intimately related to this worthy family, either by blood ties or marriage relationship.

During the past twelve months this important matter has impressed the writer and, being requested by some of the younger men of this great Byrd family, who desired to know more about their ancestors, also being aware of the tendency with so many people to bury the history of their family with themselves, he has taken upon himself the arduous effort

to produce a work for which he is inadequate to successfully complete. While the author is alone responsible for the book, he has not wrought alone; many of the members of the family have aided him with sketches and other valuable assistance. His appreciation of this kindness he has attempted otherwise to show, but especially by publishing all that has thus been sent him, except when he had positive information that it was inaccurate.

There are several things which have induced the author to attempt and carry forward his undertaking. First, that the history of this worthy family should not be so entirely neglected and dropped and their notoriety of worth and excellence should be acknowledged and perpetuated that have existed for about two centuries past. This interest is not a mere idle curiosity, but is a natural desire of the mind to find out all that can be learned of that antiquity out of which it has come. Savages may be content to roam about amid the ruins of the houses formerly inhabited by their

greater ancestors, but civilized and enlightened men insist on prying into hidden facts and endeavoring to learn their buried history.

Again the author has felt a natural desire to learn more about his own kindred. The past he has sought to show this generation is not the past of aliens and foreigners, but of those whose blood flows in his own veins. He acknowledges a strong family feeling as a motive in his work. He believes that to be descended from worthy ancestors should prove to an honorable mind a powerful incentive to hand down to posterity a record of like worth. And he rejoices that his early life spent, in part at least, amid the simplicity and hardships of the generations of more than three score years past has enabled him to appreciate the homely virtues and sturdy valor of the true-hearted men and women who helped so much to produce the happy days in which their descendants live. Thus, as a sort of link between the not very remote past and the present, he takes great pleasure in keeping fresh the memory of

those of his kindred who have ceased from their labors—the worthy name of those Byrds who were the descendants of the early pioneers of the Byrd family of Muddy Creek, Accomack county, Virginia, of the eighteenth century. And as the family is a human family, its history thus becomes a matter of general interest to all who are concerned in learning more about our common human nature.

But the author of this history does not hope that his work will interest many others besides those of whom it treats. These, however, he hopes will enjoy it, and if it shall promote among the numerous descendants of the far away founders of the family a better acquaintance, a sincere affection, and a worthy desire to honor an honorable name, he will have his reward.

COLWELL P. BYRD,
AGED 22 YEARS.

ORIGIN OF THE BYRD FAMILY OF ACCOMACK COUNTY, VIRGINIA

TRADITION says this family traces its settlement on Muddy Creek, in Accomack county, Virginia, back to the early part of the eighteenth century. The author of this book, having very recently made diligent search among the old records of wills and deeds in the clerk's office at Accomack Court House, found the old books so mutilated and worn from age that it was a matter of impossibility to find any accurate date of their settlement in that locality; consequently the writer is under the necessity of following tradition which he has received from his ancestors relative to some facts about this worthy family which was transmitted to his father, who was born in 1777, and was handed down to him by ancestral line in his early life which

the memory of more than three score and ten years has enabled him to retain until the present time. These facts the writer desires to transmit to this generation and those who are to come. Believing that they are as reliable as anything obtainable of this buried history at this time, as there is no date setting forth the positive time of the settlement of which we are writing, we must be content with the best we can obtain. The following is the traditional record: That in the early part of the eighteenth century there came a man from the Western Shore of Virginia, whose name was Nathaniel Byrd and settled in Accomack county, Virginia, on the north side of Muddy Creek, about a half mile from its banks. The place of the old settlement the writer visited recently and found there the tomb of one of his uncles bearing the date of his birth, 1769. The exact place in Virginia from whence Nathaniel Byrd came the writer does not know, but it was from him and his posterity that this great Byrd family, of whom

he writes, has become so numerous, and it is quite evident from tradition that they are lineal descendants of William Byrd, who came from England and settled in Virginia on the James River at Westover in 1670, and inherited the estate of his uncle Thomas Stegg, of London, a goldsmith who, for a while, resided in Virginia. It is of this pedigree that the author of this work desires to give an account. He has learned from ancestral information that the Nathaniel Byrd, who is mentioned above, had two sons (who their mother was the writer does not know) their names were Jacob and Nathaniel.

The writer's mind leads him to think that his great-uncle, Jacob Byrd, was a bachelor, as there seems to be no record of his ever having a family. He has heard his father speak of him as being a young man. But the other son, Nathaniel, who was the author's grandfather, married Naomi Watson and had issue; hence this brief history and genealogy of the generation of the Byrd family of Muddy Creek,

Accomack county, Virginia, from the early part of the eighteenth century on down to the beginning of 1907.

The children of Nathaniel Byrd and Naomi (Watson) Byrd, his wife, are as follows (dates of their births in most part unknown): Major Byrd, first son of Nathaniel and Naomi Byrd, was born (date of birth unknown), and married his cousin Nancy Watson (date of marriage not known). They had issue.

Selby, the second son, married Hester Wessells. To them were born two sons and one daughter.

Rebecca, the oldest daughter of Nathaniel Byrd and Naomi, his wife, married John Bloxom. They had issue—three sons.

Elizabeth, second daughter, married Littleton Trader. They had issue, a son and two daughters.

Parker Byrd, third son of Nathaniel Byrd and Naomi Byrd, was born May 18th, 1769, and died October 18th, 1820.

Naomi Byrd, third daughter of Nathaniel

NATHANIEL J. BYRD
ODESSA, MO.

and Naomi Byrd, his wife, married Southy Northam. They had issue.

Nathaniel, the fourth son (date of birth not known), died a young man.

Johannas Byrd, father of the author of this work and fifth son of Nathaniel and Naomi Byrd, was born December 2d, 1777, and died September 8th, 1853. He married Margaret Kelly (date of marriage unknown). They had issue—two sons and one daughter. Politically he was a Whig. He thought it an honor to belong to the party which for seven years gave its life and struggles to obtain their national liberty. He served in the war of 1812 and was true to his party until death claimed him. He was a Baptist and died in the hope of his future reward.

Rachel, the fourth and youngest daughter, married Jacob Kelly, died young and left one son—William Kelly.

Daniel T. Byrd, the youngest child, son of Nathaniel Byrd and Naomi (Watson) Byrd, was born at Muddy Creek, Accomack county,

Virginia, October 30th, 1785, and died at the old homestead March 30th, 1846. He was a prominent member of the Baptist church. In politics he was a Whig and adhered to his principles strenuously. He married Nancy Gillespie (date of marriage not known). They had issue—a son and daughter.

The author of this work, having made a record of the origin of this worthy family as far back as he has any information of their worthy ancestry and numerous descendants, desires now to make a record of the genealogy of the generations that have followed them. And this is the genealogy from the third generation of the first settlers at Muddy Creek down to the present time.

Tabitha, the first child, and daughter of Major Byrd and Nancy (Watson) Byrd, was born (date of birth unknown). She married Israel Trader (date of marriage not known). They had issue — two children. Edward Trader, their only son, married a Miss Underhill and moved away. I have no further

note of him. Elizabeth, their only daughter, married Richard Kelly (date of marriage not known). To them were born three children—Tabitha, John and Richard (date of their birth not known). Mr. Kelly is dead. Mrs. Kelly is living and resides with her son, Richard Kelly.

I have no dates of Major and Nancy Byrd's family; what I write about them is from personal knowledge of them. They had seven other children, making their number eight.

Nancy, the second daughter of Major and Nancy Byrd, married George Northam a Baptist preacher, and moved to Middlesex county, Virginia, where she lived and died at an advanced age. The writer knew two of their children—Deborah, daughter and George, their son, who was also a Baptist preacher.

Sally Byrd, third daughter of Major Byrd and Nancy, his wife, married Edmund Northam, brother of George, and moved to Urbanna, Middlesex county, Virginia. Four children were the result of their union. Annie,

the oldest daughter of Edmund and Sally (Byrd) Northam, married John Anthon, a lumber dealer, who resided for a while in Baltimore. Jane, the second daughter, married Lewis Bristow of Urbanna, Va., in 1847, and went from Baltimore to Urbanna to live. Sally, the youngest daughter, and Edmund, the son of Edmund and Sally Northam, the writer cannot now make any note of, except that they lived in Baltimore in 1847.

Margaret, the fourth daughter of Major and Nancy Byrd, married Thomas Kelly. Five children were the result of their union — Amanda, first daughter, born January 2d, 1809. Second child, son Samuel (date of birth not known), died January, 1845. Third child, Thomas (date of birth unknown). Margaret, the second daughter of Thomas Kelly and Margaret (Byrd) Kelly, married John Nelson. He was a carpenter. They lived in Drummondtown, Virginia, and died there (dates all unknown). They had issue. Their children live at the place of their birth. The writer

does not know their names. Martin Kelly, the youngest son of Thomas and Margaret Kelly, lived with his mother until her death, January, 1855. He married Miss Lizzie Gibb, and died in the fall of 1880, without issue.

Henrietta, fifth daughter of Major Byrd and Nancy, his wife, married Bennet Byrd. They had issue—Elizabeth and Benjamin, both dead. Major, Jr., Harriet and Nathaniel, the three youngest of the family, all died childless.

Custis Walter Byrd, first son of Selby Byrd and Hester (Wessells) Byrd, was born at Muddy Creek, Accomack county, Virginia, August 3d, 1794. He married Keziah Taylor, daughter of Shadrack and Nancy Taylor, of Sandy Branch, Accomack county, Virginia (date of marriage unknown). Two children was the result of their union. Colmore E. Byrd, only son of Custis W. Byrd and Keziah (Taylor) Byrd, was born at Muddy Creek, Virginia, October 18th, 1817. When he was quite young he went to Baltimore and served a long apprenticeship at the blacksmith trade

and became a first-class mechanic in that branch of industry, and, when arrived at manhood, he married Miss Mary Sheldon, the daughter of James and Sarah Barnes Sheldon, of Baltimore, September 19th, 1839. She was born in Baltimore, September 12th, 1818. The result of their union was four children, all of whom were born in Baltimore.

James Edward Byrd, only son of Colmore E. and Mary (Sheldon) Byrd, was born September 1st, 1840. He was educated at the public schools and Newton University at Baltimore. He removed to Accomack county, Virginia, when a youth and was employed for some time as a recorder in the clerk's office of the county court under Mr. John W. Gillett, clerk of the court. He served nearly four years in the Confederate army; was the color-bearer of that gallant battalion of Virginia of Rhode's Brigade, D. H. Hill's Division, which at the battle of Seven Pines, stormed with the bayonet the Federal redoubt in front of the Square house on the south side of the Williams-

JAMES E. BYRD,
BALTIMORE, MD., 1907.

JAMES E. BYRD,
OF CONFEDERATE ARMY, 1862.

burg pike, was the first to leap into the ditch and climbing up the muddy embankment on his hands and knees, waved the colors of the battalion over the ten brass 12 pound guns of the celebrated Empire Battery of New York. Four of his color guards, stalwart mountaineers from the peaks of Otter falling, killed and wounded, around him. The commanding officer, Captain Otey of Liberty, Virginia, died at his side, his last words: "Byrd, my boy, rally the men." In this charge his cousin, Thomas C. Kelly, was shot through the left lung in two places and lay on the field of battle all night. The awful loss of the battalion was such that but thirty-two men, under the command of Capt. John R. Bagby, of King and Queen county, were with the colors at night. It was to the remnant of the battalion and the guns captured that Jefferson Davis and Gen. R. E. Lee rode up to as the battle ceased at dark. He was, later, color-bearer of the 3d Virginia Infantry, Wise's Brigade; then exchanged into the cavalry service, and in the

campaign of 1864 was first Sergeant of Company C, 24, 5th Virginia Cavalry, General Gray's Brigade, and rode at the head of the charging squadron of that gallant regiment. In the fall and winter of 1864, he scouted for General Longstreet and General Gray and won high commendation for his services.

At the close of the war, in 1865, he returned to his native home, Baltimore, and engaged in the steamboat business and still pursues that manner of occupation.

On the 28th day of October, 1869, he married Catherine A. Fletcher, the daughter of Wm. G. and Esther A. Fletcher, of Baltimore. He has been for a number of years employed in business with the Old Bay Line Steamboat Company of Baltimore, and is at this time agent and cashier for the same. They live in Baltimore, 1724 Bolton street. They have issue—Fletcher Lee Byrd, born July 17th, 1872, who is freight soliciting agent for the Baltimore Steamboat Company. Walter Custis Byrd, born July 11th, 1879, is a clerk with

the B. & O. R. R. Co. Norral Edgar Byrd, the third and youngest son of James Edward and Catherine A. (Fletcher) Byrd, was born November 7th, 1882. He is a medical student. All of James E. Byrd's sons were born in Baltimore.

Sarah K. Byrd, oldest daughter of Colmore E. Byrd and Mary, his wife, was born in Baltimore, March 5th, 1842, and married Dr. W. J. H. Wallop of Accomack county, Virginia, November 7th, 1861, and died in Horntown, Va., July 17th, 1885. She left four children—John Douglas Wallop, Mary Byrd Wallop, Sallie Holland Wallop, and Lallie, the youngest daughter, who lived with her uncle in Baltimore. She is married and now resides in Baltimore county. Her husband is a lawyer; I do not know the name. All of Dr. Wallop's children were born at Horntown, Virginia.

Mary Ann Byrd, second daughter of Colmore E. and Mary Byrd, was born in Baltimore, August 4th, 1846. She married George

D. Evans, a farmer in Horntown, Virginia, June 6th, 1877. They have issue — Essie Evans, daughter (date of birth not known). Elizabeth Jane Byrd, youngest daughter of Colmore E. Byrd and Mary Byrd, was born February 26th, 1849. She is unmarried and lives with her brother in Baltimore.

Colmore E. Byrd died in Baltimore, September 5th, 1890. Mary (Sheldon) Byrd, his wife, who preceded him in death about twenty years, died July 2d, 1867.

Hester Ann Byrd, the only daughter of Custis W. Byrd and Keziah (Taylor) Byrd, was born at Muddy Creek, February 2d, 1817. She was left motherless almost from infancy. She grew up under the tender care of her grandmother, Nancy Taylor. She was married to Elijah Kelly, November 8th, 1834. Her husband, Elijah Kelly, was born December 5th, 1807. They had issue—Thomas C. Kelly, oldest son of Elijah Kelly and Hester Ann (Byrd) Kelly, was born August 20th, 1840. He enlisted in Company K, 34th Vir

ginia Regiment Infantry, Wise's Brigade, Bushrod Johson's Division, Longstreet's Corps, Army of Northern Virginia, April 22d, 1861; was twice wounded at the battle of Seven Pines and Fair Oaks Station on York River and Richmond Railroad, on May 31st, 1862. He lingered with these wounds until December 18th, 1862, when he returned to his command and served to the end of the war, surrendering with Gen. Robert E. Lee at Appomattox Court House on April 13th, 1865.

Elijah Kelly and his wife Hester Ann (Byrd) Kelly, had another son, Elijah Kelly, Jr., (date of his birth unknown). He went West.

Elijah Kelly, Sr., and his good wife lived a quiet life on their farm near Hallwood from the time of their marriage until their death at a ripe old age. Mr. Kelly died June 15th, 1892. His wife preceded him in death seven years, dying June the 8th, 1885. Their son, Thomas C. Kelly, lives in Hallwood, Accomack county, Virginia, and is Commissioner of Revenue.

Custis W. Byrd had other children by his second marriage with Mary Fisher, daughter of Fairfax and Sallie Fisher. John Washington Custis Byrd, oldest son of Custis W. Byrd and Mary (Fisher) Byrd, was born at Muddy Creek, Accomack county, Virginia, May 7th, 1826. He went to Baltimore about the year 1848 or 1849, and was employed in the agricultural implement manufacturing establishment of Sinclair & Co., on Light street, near Lombard. Later on in life he married and settled in Baltimore and engaged in the wood and coal business, and continued that business until his failing health compelled him to retire from active work and finally resulted in his death on March 1st, 1901. He had issue. John W. Byrd, first son, who is a coal dealer in Baltimore; and Charles W. Byrd, his second son, who also lives in Baltimore. His widow survives him and resides in South Baltimore.

Sylvester Byrd, second son of Custis W. Byrd and Mary, his wife, was born in 1828.

He was a carpenter and unmarried, and died March 7th, 1901, in the 73d year of his age. Priscella Byrd, born 1827, married Abednego Taylor, and died October 16th, 1889. Mary E. C. Byrd, born 1830, married James Miles, of Accomack county, Virginia, and died September 28th, 1859. Odien J. Byrd, third son of Custis W. and Mary Byrd, was born June 12th, 1832. He is now in the 75th year of his age. He is a carpenter by trade, but owing to infirmities of age and failing health has retired from active life. He married Allameda Parker, June 3d, 1858, daughter of Mr. Parker and Mary Jane Parker, of Baltimore.

The children of Odien J. Byrd and Allameda (Parker) Byrd are: William Odien Byrd, born 1860; second child, Cora Mary, born 1863; the third child, Harry Ambrose, born 1865; the fourth child, Sallie Littlefield Byrd, born 1870; the fifth child, James Milton Byrd, born 1881. Veda Allameda, youngest child of Odien J. and Allameda

(Parker) Byrd, was born 1888. Odien J. Byrd's wife died the latter part of 1905. He now resides with his daughter, Mrs. William Hubbard, 302 East Randall street, Baltimore, Md. William A. Byrd, born 1834, lives in Harford county, Maryland.

Sallie Custis Stoakly Byrd, the youngest child of Custis W. and Mary (Fisher) Byrd, was born in Accomack county, Virginia, 1836. She married Mr. Littlefield, of Baltimore (date of marriage not known), and died July 24th, 1868.

The children of Sallie C. S. (Byrd) Littlefield are: A. S. Littlefield, of Colorado Springs, Col.; Mollie Littlefield, of Baltimore, Md.; Emma (Littlefield) Watson, of Philadelphia, Pa., and Blanch (Littlefield) North, of Philadelphia, Pa.

Colmore S. Byrd, second son of Selby Byrd and Hester Byrd, his wife, was born April 3d, 1796. The writer knew him well. He was a good man, and was of excellent service to his neighbors. If any were sick or in

sorrow about their spiritual condition, he was sent for to impart comfort and give spiritual advice. He was a deacon in the Baptist church and was liberal and charitable toward those who differed from him in their religious views, He wanted everybody to worship God according to the dictates of their own consciences. He was a model man and every one that knew him loved "Colly" Byrd, as he was called.

He married Hetty Taylor, February 3d, 1820. They lived at Muddy Creek, Accomack county, Va., until the time of his death, January, 1845. His widow still remained on their farm several years after his death. Seven children were the result of their union. First, Matilda W., born April 1st, 1821, and died in infancy. The second child, William S. Byrd, oldest son of Colmore S. Byrd and Hetty (Taylor) Byrd, was born at Muddy Creek, June 7th, 1822. He was educated in the ordinary country school of his day obtaining a fair business education

and being possessed with a business capacity in early life he entered into the mercantile trade and was prosperous. In December, 1816, he was married to Mary Bloxom, of New Church, Va. To them were born one child, William F. Byrd (date of birth unknown), he lives in Norfolk, Va.

William S. Byrd's first wife died soon after the birth of their son, William F. (I do not know the date of her death.) In due course of time he was married to his second wife, who was Miss Mollie Broughton, of Temperanceville, Va., the result of this union was two children, daughter and son. Fannie, the first child, married and died, (I do not know the date of her marriage or death.) Milton J., the son, is married and doing business in Baltimore and resides there. William S. Byrd still continued his business at Oak Hall, Accomack county, Va., with moderate success for several years until advanced age and failing health caused him to retire and move to Baltimore, where he died August 14th,

1888. His widow still survives him and lives with her son in Baltimore.

Abednego, second son of Colmore S. and Hetty Byrd, was born February 27th, 1825, and died August 9th, 1843. Solomon C., third son, born June 19th, 1827, died August 12th, 1828.

Burnata, second daughter, born January 24th, 1829, and died in infancy. Ansemos S. Byrd, fourth son of Colmore S. Byrd and Hetty, his wife, was born October 26th, 1830. He was educated in the country schools and obtained a good business education. When quite young he engaged in the mercantile business, which he pursued all his life. When a young man he married Miss Ellen S. James, a young lady of culture and excellent refinement (date of marriage not known). They lived in Mappsville, Accomack county, Va. He continued business there until his death. The result of their marriage was four children—Emma, Ida, Upshur and Nellie (date of their births not known). Emma, first

daughter of Ausemos S. and Ellen S. (James) Byrd, married Nehemiah Nock, of the noted Nock family of Sea Side, Va. They have six children. Their names are Medora, Josie, Hattie, Ernest, Mildred and Constance. Ida, the second daughter of A. S. and Ellen S, Byrd, married Eugene Mason (date of marriage unknown). They have two children— Ethel and Marva. Upshur Byrd, the only son of Ausemos S. and Ellen S. Byrd, has one son, named Marion. Nellie, youngest child of Ausemos S. Byrd and Ellen S. Byrd, I have no note of. Henry S., the fifth son of Colmore S. and Hetty Byrd, was born February 7th, 1834, and died in infancy.

Albert F. Byrd, sixth son of Colmore S. Byrd and Hetty, his wife, was born at Muddy Creek, June 30th, 1835. He received a fair country education in the days of his boyhood and youth. He adapted himself to farming and later on became a practical farmer. On April 27th, 1858, he married Miss Charlotte E. Matthews, a lady of mild disposi-

tion and fine attainments, the daughter of Stoakly and Susan (Mapp) Matthews of Temperanceville, Va. Together with his farming interests, he devoted a part of his time to the fire and life insurance agency. He was a prominent member of the Methodist Episcopal Church, South, as were all his brothers. He and his good wife are both dead and gone to their rest. They left four sons, who fill prominent business positions in life. Lynn C. Byrd, their first son, was born March 19th, 1859, and preceded his father in death about three months. He married Miss Ella McCullough, of Port Deposit (date of marriage unknown) and was engaged in the drug business in that city from his youth up to the time of his death, which occurred July, 1901. and left his widow a nice estate.

Clyde P. Byrd, the second son, was born June 9th, 1861. He married Miss Ada Baily, of Baltimore (date of marriage not known). He is engaged in the brokerage business in Baltimore and lives at Catonsville, Md.

They have four children. I do not know the dates of their birth. Their names are Caryl, Clyde Wilson, Lynn C. and Evelyn Byrd.

Colmore Ernest Byrd, the third son of Albert F. and Charlotte E. Byrd, was born January 22d, 1868. He devoted a few years in his early manhood to teaching school in his native town, Temperanceville, Va. In 1895 he engaged in business with the wholesale drug firm of James Baily & Son, in Baltimore. On the 26th day of June, 1896, he married Miss Mary Virginia Gillespie, the daughter of Albert J. and Catherine (Dix) Gillespie, of Temperanceville, Accomack county, Va. They have one child, only daughter, Evelyn Louise Byrd, born at Temperanceville, Va., September 14th, 1899. He continued his business in Baltimore about 11 years, during which time he purchased a nice farm, a suburban home at Pocomoke City and moved with his family from their home in Virginia to his new purchase; and in 1906 he retired from the drug business and accepted the position of cashier of the

DR. OSCAR F. BYRD,
PORTSMOUTH, VA.

EVELYN BLANCHE BYRD, BORN JULY 1ST, 1905
DAUGHTER OF DR. OSCAR FRANKLIN BYRD
AND ANNIE BLANCHE BYRD

Citizens National Bank of Pocomoke City, Md., and is also one of the directors of the same. In a personal matter the writer assumes the privilege to say of Mr. Byrd that he is a true type of a Southern gentleman, a strict business man, a consistent and prominent member of the Methodist Protestant church.

Dr. Oscar F. Byrd, youngest son of Albert F. Byrd and Charlotte E. (Matthews) Byrd, was born at Temperanceville, Va., March 4th, 1870. In his early life he applied himself to study with the view of gaining a profession, and in early manhood he entered the Dental Schools of the University of Maryland, in Baltimore; graduated there in 1890, and began the practice of his profession on November 20th, 1901. He married Miss Annie Blanche Richards, the only daughter of J. James and Hattie A. (Brittingham) Richards of Pocomoke City, Md. They live in Portsmouth, Va., where he practices dentistry. They have one child, Evelyn Byrd, born July 1st, 1905.

Henry E. Byrd, the only surviving and

youngest son of Colmore S. Byrd and Hetty (Taylor) Byrd, was born January 29th, 1841. He married Martha J. Matthews, December 23d, 1862, the daughter of George P. and Martha Matthews, both of whom were prominent members of the Methodist Episcopal church. The children of Henry E. Byrd and Martha, his wife, are: Edith Lee Byrd, eldest daughter, was born Nov. 11, 1863; Otho West Byrd, born October 31st, 1866; Lillian Olivia Byrd, born August 4th, 1869, and died September 24th, 1872. Lillian Olivia Byrd, 2d, the youngest daughter of Henry E. and Martha (Matthews) Byrd, was born October 21st, 1878.

I am personally acquainted with Henry E. Byrd, and will, by permission, mention some personalities of him, characteristic of his early business life. For a number of years he divided his time between farming and mercantile trade, He is quick and prompt in all his movements and of great energy. For many years a successful traveling salesman; later in

life a successful merchant in Temperanceville, Va., up to a disastrous fire in 1903, in which he lost most of the savings of his life. But he and his son Otho, with promptness and redoubled energy, rebuilt and started a successful business by the help of friends, liberal discounts of creditors and the Masonic fraternity, of which they both are members. He and his family are all members of the Methodist Episcopal church, South, and, I think, his politics are Democratic. He is also a great sportsman, and is styled the Nimrod of this great Byrd family.

Enatia Byrd, the only daughter of Selby Byrd, and Hester (Wessells) Byrd, was born at Muddy Creek, Accomack county, Va., April 4th, 1799. She married Daniel Boston, of Shelltown, Somerset county, Md., in October, 1819, a worthy young man and prosperous farmer. She was a lady of bright intellect and fine attainments for usefulness. She was modest and domestic in her manner of life, kind and benevolent in her deeds. Her

Christian character was of a high standard. In her early life she made a profession of religion and united with the Baptist church. She magnified her profession by her consistent and loving devotion to the cause of her Lord. She was prominent in the organization of the Rehoboth Baptist Church in Somerset county, Maryland, and was one of the very few charter members that constituted that little church about the year 1839 or 1840, of which she was a faithful supporter, both spiritually and financially, until her death, which occurred on the 11th of June, 1864. The church has become a great power for good in that community.

Mrs. Boston and her husband both lived to a ripe old age and were members of the Rehoboth Baptist Church at their death. They left one son, Solomon Charles Boston, their only child born August 23d, 1820. He was trained to farm life and reared with the care of devoted parents. He was a model boy, judging from the manner of his manly and Christian life as

we knew him later on. About the age of sixteen years he made a profession of religion, honored his profession by his consistent course in life, and united with the Baptist church of which his parents were members. Up to this time of his life he had made use of the country schools to the best advantage he could derive from them, with the view of a higher education and more permanent usefulness in life. A. about the age of eighteen years he entered the Seminary in Richmond, Va., now Richmond College, where he received his ministerial education and became a very prominent and efficient preacher of the Baptist denomination. He began his arduous labors in the gospel ministry quite young with the one purpose— the glory of God and the salvation of souls- He married Mrs. Mary Ann Nock (nee Marshall) the young widow of Mr. Gillette Nock, a young man of popular fame, about the year 1846 (the exact date of marriage is not known). She was born near Oak Hall, Accomack county, Va., October 26th, 1822. She was of

true Virginian type, a lady of high Christian standard and was an excellent helpmeet to her husband. They walked together in the ordinances and commandments of their Lord with the one object in view: to declare the gospel of the Son of God to all whom they could reach. Mr. Boston preached as missionary on the Eastern Shore of Maryland and Virginia for several years, during which time he organized a Baptist church at Vienna, Dorchester county, Md., and preached for his mother church, at Rehoboth, at the same time, and at different school house stations in the country. He also preached in Northampton and Accomack counties a part of the time during this period of his life.

In 1851 he founded the First Baptist Church of Pocomoke City, and was its first pastor, in the latter part of 1857. He resigned his pastorate there and accepted a call to the Second Baptist Church, in Petersburg, Va., and having finished his work there in 1861, he accepted a call to the Farmville Baptist

Church, in Virginia. During his stay there the war between the States became so troublesome that he resigned his charge in 1862, and ventured, with his wife and son, then a lad, to run the blockade across the Chesapeake Bay in a canoe, and succeeded in reaching the home of his parents in Somerset county, Maryland, who were then very feeble and remained with them sometime. Subsequently he accepted a call to Lee Street Baptist Church, in Baltimore. During his pastorate there his wife died, on the 15th day of April, 1869. Soon after the death of his wife he resigned his charge in Baltimore and accepted a call in 1870 to the Baptist church in Frenchtown, N. J. In 1872 he married his second wife—Miss Mary E. Britton, of that town, a very accomplished lady, and moved to Brewington, King and Queen county, Va., and served the church there for several years; then returned to Eastern Shore again and was pastor of the Baptist church at Onancock, Accomack county, Va., until the latter part

of 1883, when he accepted a call to the First Baptist Church of Pocomoke City, his former charge, and continued there until his death, which occurred on the 15th day of June, 1887, in the 68th year of his age. Thus the Rev. Solomon Charles Boston finished his life work near the place where he began it. His children are as follows:

His son Francis R. Boston, the only child of his first marriage with Mrs. Mary Ann Nock, was born at Shelltown, Somerset county, Md., December 29th, 1847. In his boyhood he was placed in good schools at different localities where his father was called to preach. With great care his parents endeavored to prepare him for a useful life. I think he finished his preparation in the town of Princess Anne, Somerset county, Md., for a college course, and in early life he entered the Columbian College in Washington, D. C., where he received his ministerial education and graduated there with distinction and was set apart to the gospel ministry and

REV. SOLOMON C. BOSTON
SOMERSET CO., MD.

preached in many different places in Virginia and Atlanta, Ga., and is now the Rev. F. R. Boston, D. D., pastor of the Baptist church at Warrington, Va. About the year 1875 he married Miss Ann Schoolfield, of Petersburg, Va., and had issue: Mela May Boston, only daughter of Rev. F. R. Boston, and Ann (Schoolfield) Boston, who married Edward Spillman Turner, a lawyer in Warrington, Fauquier county, Va. (date of marriage not known). They have issue: Anne Schoolfield Turner and Ellen Lovell Turner. Chase Schoolfield Boston, the only son of Rev. F. R. Boston and Ann Boston, his wife, is a prosperous druggist in Washington, D. C. The Rev. Solomon C. Boston had other children by his second marriage with Miss Mary E. Britton, of New Jersey. Their names are, Mr. Charles Daniel Boston, of Baltimore, Md., and Miss Belle Boston, of Fauquier county, Virginia. The Rev. Solomon C. Boston, his children, grandchildren and great grandchildren are all descendants

of the Byrd family who first settled in Accomack county, Virginia, in the early part of 1700, on the mother's side of the family, Mrs. Enatia (Byrd) Boston, who was born at Muddy Creek, Va., April 4th, 1799, and died at her home near Shelltown, Somerset county, Md., June 11th, 1864.

Rebecca Byrd, the oldest daughter of Nathaniel and Naomi (Watson) Byrd, married John Bloxom (date of marriage not known). They had issue, their children being as follows: Woodman Bloxom, the oldest son of John and Rebecca (Byrd) Bloxom, was born in Accomack county, Virginia (date of birth unknown). He was a blacksmith, served his apprenticeship in his native county, and when a young man he went to Philadelphia, married and remained there until his death. He had issue, three children—Woodman, Ann and Rebecca, all of Philadelphia, where I visited them in 1853. John Bloxom, the second son, also went to Philadelphia when a young man and married

a lady from Smyrna, Del. I do not remember her name nor the date of marriage. He died young and left one son, John Bloxom. I have no further trace of him. Selby, the third and youngest son of John and Rebecca (Byrd) Bloxom, married Polly Copes, of Accomack county, Virginia. I am not certain as to his occupation, but I think he was a farmer. They had issue, three daughters—Elizabeth, Mary and Rebecca. Mary married a Mr. Jacobs, a tailor by trade. They lived in Accomack county, Virginia (after the death of their father) with their mother until about 1845, then moved to New York. I met them in Philadelphia in 1853, while they were there on a visit to relatives, and have not heard from them since.

Elizabeth Byrd, the second daughter of Nathaniel and Naomi Byrd, was born at Muddy Creek, Va., about the year 1667 (exact date of birth not known). She married Littleton Trader (date of marriage unknown). They had issue, three children—

Samuel, Tabitha and Ann. Samuel married and lived between Accomack county, Virginia, and Worcester county, Maryland, and had issue, five sons—Samuel, Littleton, William, Edward and James, and one daughter, Ann, who married a man in Philadelphia named Wood, and died there, leaving one son, William Wood. I do not know anything more of them.

Selby Byrd, the oldest son of Parker Byrd and Keziah (Gillespie) Byrd, was born December 23d, 1807. He grew up with his parents on the farm at Muddy Creek. At the close of his school days his mind was naturally turned to some occupation in life by which he might secure a livelihood. His choice of business inclined him to the water and very early in life he took to a commercial line of trade and soon became a skillful officer and commander of a grain and produce schooner which plied between Muddy Creek and Baltimore for several years, and traded in the commodities of that vicinity.

He married Amanda Kelley, February 2d, 1839, and continued in his chosen business a few years after his marriage, when he abandoned his commercial life and took to farming, in which he continued with moderate success until the close of the war between the States. About that time he began a successful and prosperous general merchandise business by which he accumulated a nice estate and continued in that business until his death, which occurred on April 3d, 1880. His wife, Amanda Byrd, preceded him in death a little more than a year, having died March 7th, 1879. Their children are: Clarissa Byrd, the first daughter of Selby and Amanda (Kelley) Byrd was born January 7th, 1840. She married Major Bloxom (date of marriage not known) and died August 4th, 1878.

Harriet D. Byrd, second daughter, was born September 30th, 1842. Mary F. Byrd, third daughter, was born April 5th, 1845. Thomas S. Byrd, the only son of Selby Byrd and Amanda, his wife, was born March 2d, 1847,

and died April 6th, 1895. His children are: first, E. Roy, born March 16th, 1878; second, Edward M., born July 13th, 1883; third, Annie A., born November 29th, 1884; fourth, E. Ruth, born October 27th, 1888; fifth, Thomas S., the youngest child, was born March 23d, 1895, and died March 8th, 1901.

Margaret J. Byrd, the youngest child of Selby and Amanda Byrd, was born September 15th, 1852, and was married to William R. Byrd, of Accomack county, Virginia, December 15th, 1870. Later on they moved to Baltimore, where he engaged in a mercantile business, and still continues this occupation there. They had issue: Pearla K. Byrd, first child, born December 16th, 1873, and died January 26th, 1892; Blanche, the second child, died in infancy.

Harriet D. Byrd, second daughter of Selby Byrd and Amanda (Kelley) Byrd, married John N. Watson September 17th, 1866. They have four children: Thomas N. Watson, born July 25th, 1867; Mary C. Watson, born

April 24th, 1870; Theodocia Ernestine Watson, born March 5th, 1872; and John Selby Watson, born May 6th, 1874. They are all of Temperanceville, Accomack county, Va. Mary F. Byrd, the third daughter of Selby and Amanda Byrd, was born at Muddy Creek, Accomack county, Virginia, April 5th, 1845. She married Reuben Sapp, the son of Andrew and Lavenia Sapp of Kent county, Delaware on the 18th of January, 1869, and the following spring they moved to the northern part of Illinois and engaged in farming there for 17 years, after which they returned to Kent county, Delaware, and lived a retired life until his death, which occured on August 26th, 1904. He was a God-fearing man and a law-abiding citizen. In his religious-views he was a Quaker. He left no children. His widow survives him and resides in Harrington, Del.

Matilda Byrd, the oldest daughter of Parker and Keziah Byrd, was born 1809 (the exact date not known). She married Samuel S. Lucas, November, 1825. They

had issue, three children—Henry P. Lucas, first son, born September 10th, 1826, and died in Brooklyn, N. Y., unmarried, about 1850; Sylvanus H. Lucas, second son, was born March 10th, 1834. He lives in Baltimore and is doing business there. Sallie A. Lucas, the only daughter of Samuel S. and Matilda (Byrd) Lucas, was born August 1st, 1836, and died in 1860.

Sallie Byrd, the youngest daughter of Parker Byrd and Keziah, his wife, was born in 1811. She married Solomon Small (date of marriage not known). They had five children—Marcellus, Sylvasten, Elizabeth, John and Matilda. I have no record of their births.

Richard P. Byrd, the second son and fourth child of Parker Byrd and Keziah Byrd (nee Gillespie), was born at Muddy Creek, March 4th, 1813. He was brought up to farm life and followed that occupation all through his days. When he was a young man he was employed as supervisor of large farming

interests in Accomack county, Virginia (his native place). He was a practical farmer and continued in his employment as supervisor until his marriage with Nancy J. Parks, the daughter of Edward Parks, of Leemont, Va., March 1st, 1843, after which he settled on his own farm, where he was born, and remained there a number of years, and then moved to a farm that his wife had inherited from her father, near Parksley. He continued there until his death, July 4th, 1881.

Their children were all born at Muddy Creek, Accomack county, Va. Their names are as follows: Burnetta S. Byrd, oldest daughter of Richard P. and Nancy (Parks) Byrd, was born February 14th, 1844, who married A. M. Rew, who died and left no children; Edward P. Byrd, the oldest son, was born September 12th, 1845. He was educated in the plain country schools of his neighborhood and acquired a sufficient scholastic training for a practical life and applied himself to farming. He has been successful

and owns valuable real estate in Accomack county. He married Miss Sallie E. Bundick, November 27th, 1878, the daughter of John A. and Elizabeth (Parks) Bundick. They live near Metompkin, Va., and have no children.

Winfield Scott Byrd, the second son of Richard P. and Nancy J. Byrd, was born October 7th, 1847. He received a limited education in home schools and prepared himself for farm life. He married Miss Bettie Mason about the 20th (?) of March, 1872 (?) and settled on his farm near Parksley, Va. They have one child only, a daughter— Nanie R. Byrd, born January 5th, 1873.

Charles L. Byrd, third son of Richard P. Byrd and Nancy J., his wife, was born June 6th, 1849. He is a thrifty business man and doing a prosperous general merchandise business at Metompkin, Accomack county, Va. He married Miss M. V. Bundick, the daughter of John A. and Elizabeth Bundick (nee Parks) October 13th, 1875. Just here

I will mention the fact that Charles L. Byrd's wife and Edward P. Byrd's wife are sisters, and are the daughters of Elizabeth Bundick (nee Parks), who was the daughter of John D. Parks, a wealthy real estate owner and a well-known citizen in Accomack county.

The children of Charles L. and M. V. Byrd (nee Bundick) are as follows: William W., first son, was born at Metomkin, Va., December, 24th, 1882; Charles W., second son, was born May 9th, 1886—he is now at the University Medical College of Richmond, Va., and expects to graduate in the medical profession in 1907; John A. Byrd, the third son, of Charles L. Byrd and M. V., his wife, was born September 6th, 1888—he is at Richmond College taking a law course; Aaron S. Byrd, the youngest son of C. L. and M. V. (Bundick) Byrd, was born June 6th, 1894. He is at home with his parents.

Cynthia E. Byrd, the youngest daughter and fifth child of Richard P. and Nancy J. Byrd, born September 15th, 1851. She is the

wife of Frank T. Rew, and has two sons—the Hon. John R. Rew, born February 12th, 1873, and J. Harry Rew, born September 17th, 1877. They are both lawyers and practicing in the courts at Accomack Court House, Va.

John T. Byrd, the sixth and youngest child of Richard P. Byrd and Nancy J. (Parks) Byrd, was born August 5th, 1856. He married Miss Maggie Mason (date of marriage not known), died February 7th, 1897. His widow and three children survive him. The children's names are Richard P., Belvia and Mason Byrd. I have no record of their births. They live in Baltimore.

The above data and genealogy of Richard P. and Nancy J. Byrd, his wife, and family were furnished me by Charles L. Byrd, one of their sons, now living at Metompkin, Va., and he says that his father died July 4th, 1881, at the age of sixty-eight years and four months. His widow survives him and is now at the advanced age of about eighty-three (?)

years and lives at Parksley, Accomack county, Va.

John E. Byrd, the youngest child of Parker and Keziah (Gillespie) Byrd, (date of his birth unknown). He went to Philadelphia when a young man and married. I have no further trace of him

Naomi, the third daughter of Nathaniel, the second, and Naomi (Watson) Byrd, his wife, was born about January 20th (?) 1776 (?). She married Southy Northam about February 14th, (?) 1804. They had issue, five children—Lucretia, first daughter, born March 10th, (?) 1805. She married Meshach Duncan March 5th, 1825. They had issue. Their first child, William Duncan, born December 26th, 1825, is now in the eighty-second year of his age and lives at Temperanceville, Accomack county, Va. He has been an active and consistent member of the Baptist church for about three score years and has not lost the vital spark yet in his Master's service. Elizabeth A., the sec-

ond child and oldest daughter of Meshach and Lucretia (Northam) Duncan, was born November 2d, 1827. Gillett, the oldest son and second child of Southy Northam and Naomi (Bryd) Northam, was born about November 10th (?), 1806 (?). He married Betsy Cocke about 1833 (?). Their children are; first, Polly, who married Gilbert Ross and had issue—Levin and David. Levin married Miss Burnetta Godwin. They live at Hallwood, Va. The second child of Gillett and Betsy (Cocke) Northam—David—married Eugenia Godwin. The third—Annie—married Sylvester Johnson. Rachel, third child of Southy Northam and Naomi, his wife, married Meshach Fisher. Their children were Harriet, John D., Samuel, Sarah, and Burnetta Ann. The youngest child of Southy and Naomi (Bryd) Northam married Benjamin Byrd. They both died on their farm at Messongo (date of death unknown). They left no children.

The following is the genealogical record of

Johannas Byrd and his family, the fourth son of Nathaniel and Naomi (Watson) Byrd. He was born December 2d, 1777, and died September 8th, 1853, and was twice married. His descendants are numerous. His first marriage was with Miss Margaret Kelley, about the year 1805. She was the daughter of Jacob Kelley, of near Johnson's store, Accomack county, Virginia. She was born about 1785, and died in November, 1813. His second marriage was with Miss Elana Cocke in 1816. She was born September 19th, 1792, and died October 3d, 1842. She was the daughter of Richard Cocke, of Accomack county, Virginia, and was a lineal descendant of the noted Cocke family of England.

The children of Johannas and Margaret (Kelley) Byrd are—Selby, first son, who was born at Muddy Creek, Accomack county, Va., July 16th, 1806. He was educated for a teacher at the academy, then open at Pungoteague, Va. After finishing his education he began the work of training young minds

in literature. He taught in several places and in 1833 (?) he went to Somerset county, Maryland, and taught at the place now known as Kingston. In 1834 he married Miss Amelia Lankford, a young lady of that locality, and died about September, 1835, and leaving one child, which soon followed him in death.

Jacob K., the second son, was born April 29th, 1809. He grew up with his parents on the farm and applied himself to that occupation all his life. About the 15th of April, 1847, he married Miss Susan Fisher, the daughter of Henry and Betsy (Northam) Fisher. The result of their union was four children—William S., the first son of Jacob K. and Susan (Fisher) Byrd, was born January 19th, 1848. He resides on his father's homestead. He married Sallie E. Byrd October 6th, 1869. Their children are Emily E., born May 20th, 1870, and Martin Thomas, born July 26th, 1871, and died August 30th, 1878.

Johannas F. Byrd, second son of Jacob K. and Susan Byrd, was born in Accomack county, Virginia, August 31st, 184 (?). He received a meagre education and adapted himself to farm life. He married Miss Mary A. Martin September 4th, 1873. They have issue—Mattie A., first child, daughter, born April 13th, 1875. She is holding a prominent position in business life in Philadelphia. The second child, infant girl, born September 1st, 1876; third child, infant boy, born February 9th, 1879. Both died in infancy.

Clarence E. Byrd, the fourth and youngest child of Johannas F. and Mary A. (Martin) Byrd, was born August 26th, 1889. He is receiving his education at the High School in Pocomoke City. His father is a successful farmer in Worcester county, Maryland, and lives at Goodwill, four miles from Pocomoke City.

Elizabeth M., the oldest daughter of Jacob K. and Susan Byrd, was born May 13th, 1854. She married John William Byrd (date

of marriage unknown). They have issue—Thomas J. Byrd, first child of John William and Elizabeth M. Byrd, was born June 12th, 1882. Cecia A., the second, was born August 14th, 1885. Onie S., youngest child of John William and Elisabeth M. Byrd, was born October 8th, 1892. They live at Hallwood, Va., and are engaged in a manufacturing enterprise and industry.

Annie S., the youngest daughter of Jacob K. Byrd and Susan (Fisher) Byrd, was born April 5th, 1860. She married Parker Kelley, son of George and Elisabeth A. Kelley, of Messongo, Accomack county, Va. They have issue. The first child, Byrd P., born September 9th, 1885; second, Martin J., born August 10th, 1889; the thirl, Joseph A., born March 8th, 1892; fourth, George E., born January 3d, 1895; fifth, Elsie A., born November 18th, 1896; William J., sixth and youngest child of Parker and Annie S. Kelley (nee Byrd), was born at Messongo, Va., April 5th, 1899.

Hetty, the first daughter of Johannas and Margaret Byrd (nee Kelley), was born at Muddy Creek, Va., September 1st, 1811. She married Smith Cutler, a carpenter of Messongo, Va., in the early part of 1834. They had issue. Their first child, Margaret Ann, was born January 12th (?), 1835, and died in 1839. John S. Cutler, the second child of Smith and Hetty Cutler, was born at Messongo, Accomack county, Va. As he grew up into boyhood and youth, and having the spirit of energy and ambition, he naturally sought to acquaint himself with some line of work by which he could obtain a livelihood. His mind being turned to the carpenter's trade, he engaged in that calling and devoted his time to improving himself in that pursuit until 1861, when the war between the States came on, when he joined the Confederate army and served until the close of the war under Gen. Robert E. Lee, and was with him in the Battle of Gettysburg. After the close of the war, in 1865, he returned

to his home in Accomack county, Va., and resumed his work at the carpenter's bench. On April 26th, 1866, he married Miss Rebecca Hall, the daughter of Thomas and Sallie (Drummond) Hall. He continued to follow his chosen occupation until a few years ago, when he sold his property in Virginia and moved to Salisbury, Md., where he and his good wife are living retired lives. They have several children, of whom I have no record. I think that they are all married.

Ann Eliza, the third child of Smith Cutler and Hetty (Byrd) Cutler, was born about January, 1838 (?). She married Oliver Bunting. Alexander S., the fourth child, went to New Orleans and engaged in the paint business. I have no further trace of him. George, the fifth child, was born about October, 1846. He, I think, is a farmer, and lives somewhere in Virginia. Mrs. Cutler was a godly woman. The life she lived on earth was evidenced by her faith in the Son of God. She was a sweet singer in Israel,

WM. BYRD NORTHAM, SR.
CHESTER, PA.

MARY E. NORTHAM
CHESTER, PA.

and honored her Lord with her voice. She was a consistent and devoted member of the Old School Baptist Church, and was faithful in her Master's service until death called her to her reward in heaven in 1848, not long after the birth of her youngest son, William.

Peggy Byrd, the second daughter of Johannas and Margaret Byrd, was born November 25th, 1813, and died quite young. I have no record of date of death.

Johannas Byrd's children of his second marriage with Elana Cocke are as follows: first, infant boy (dead); second child, Margaret, was born May 28th, 1819, and died July 2d, 1893. She married William C. Northam, of Accomack county, Virginia, in December, 1847. He was a carpenter by trade. The result of their union was seven children: The first son, William Byrd Northam, was born October 1st, 1848. When a young man he went to Phœnixville, Pa., and engaged in the moulding business. On April the 28th, 1875, he was married to Mary Elizabeth

Spare. She was born December 24th, 1853, in Montgomery county, Pennsylvania. They have issue—first child, George Valentine Northam, born August 15th, 1876. He is a machinist by trade, is married and now lives in Lorain, Ohio. Harry Spare, second son, born November 18th, 1877, electrician, is married and living in Lorain, Ohio. William Byrd Northam, Jr., born July 27th, 1879, attorney at law, and practices his profession in Chester, Pa. He is unmarried and lives at home with his parents. Ella, fourth child, born February 14th, 1881, married Alfred C. Thorpe, both of Chester, Pa. John Albert, fifth child, born April 11th, 1884; he is a steel moulder, is married and resides now in Chester, Pa.

Margaret May, sixth child, born April 6th, 1886, married John Henry Ruch. They live at Sharon Hill, Del county, Pennsylvania.

Elsie, the seventh child, born March 1st, 1888, is living at home with her parents.

Emily Jane, eighth child, born August 24th, 1891.

Charles Byrd Northam, ninth and youngest child of William B. and Mary Elizabeth (Spare) Northam, of Chester, Pa., was born April 23d, 1895.

Mary A., oldest daughter of William C. and Margaret (Byrd) Northam, was born October 31st, 1849. She married John W. Groton (date of marriage not known). He is a farmer and lives near Parksley, Accomack county, Va. They have issue.

Gillett W., third child, was born November 12th, 1851, lives at Messongo, Accomack county, Va.

Emily J., fourth child, was born December 17th, 1853. She married Peter Gillespie (date of marriage not known) and died in March, 1903, leaving three children—Mattie, John H. and Peter. I have no record of their births.

George F., fifth child, born September 13th, 1856, dead.

Martin J., sixth child, born September 26th, 1858, dead.

Henry Clay, seventh and youngest child of William Custis Northam and Margaret (Byrd) Northam, was born November 15th, 1861. He grew up in his country home with his parents and received a common country-school education. Later in life he began a mercantile business and continued with moderate success for several years. On April 13th, 1892, he married Miss S. Annie Hancock and soon after retired from mercantile life and engaged in farming. They have issue—first child, V. Margaret, born January 26th, 1893; second child, A. Ethel, born December 9th, 1894; third, Otis, born December 5th, 1898; H. Paul, fourth and youngest child of Henry Clay and Annie (Hancock) Northam, was born September 14th, 1900. They are comfortably fixed on their farm in Worcester county, Maryland, about five miles from Pocomoke City.

The children and grandchildren of William

C. and Margaret (Byrd) Northam are all descendants of the Byrd family on the mother's side of the family.

Parker Byrd, second son of Johannas Byrd and Elana (Cocke) Byrd, was born February 8th, 1821. He grew up on the farm with his parents. In early life his mind was turned to educational interest, and he made use of the best means for a preparation to instruct others that the schools of his day could afford him. He engaged in teaching for several years with general satisfaction. He was well drilled in military tactics and made an efficient officer, was unanimously elected captain in the militia in 1848, and in 1851 was promoted to the office of adjutant in the Ninety-ninth Regiment of the Virginia militia, and served under Maj.-Gen. James Northam and Col. Francis Miller with eulogistic praise. He married Mary Ann Trader in 1850, and engaged in farming and was successful in accumulating real estate. He was, in politics, an old-line Whig, until the Re-

bellion, when he became a Southern sympathizer, and after that he voted with the Democratic party. He was a conscientious man and tried to practice the "Golden Rule," being a consistent member of the Baptist Church for more than a half century. He was chairman of the building committee for the first house of worship of the Bethel Baptist Church, built at Muddy Creek in Accomack county, Virginia, in 1845. His interest in his Master's cause was unabating, and in advanced years he superintended the building of their new and commodious house of worship, built in 1887. He was honored and respected by those who knew him for his uprightness, honesty and integrity, which he adhered to until his death. He died in the triumphs of faith in his God, on the 5th day of April, 1895, in the seventy-fifth year of his age. His funeral services were held at his home and were attended by about five hundred persons. He was a good man. What better eulogy could he and his good wife

(who preceded him in death several years) have? They left seven sons, whose names are: Alexander W. Byrd, oldest son of Parker and Mary A. (Trader) Byrd, was born April 17th, 1851. He and his family reside in Baltimore.

Teakle L., the second son, was born March 31st, 1853. He married Miss Fisher (the date of marriage unknown). He is a farmer and resides on his farm in Accomack county, Virginia. They have several children. I have no record of their births.

Henry Parker, third son, was born July 17th, 1855, and died unmarried February 5th, 1907.

Staton Franklin, fourth son, was born November 19th, 1857. He married Clara J. Lucas, December 27th, 1882. They had two children, Samuel F., the oldest, born June 15th, 1887, and Elana, the second child, born August 26th, 1890. He is a farmer and general merchandise dealer at Poulson, Accomack county, Va.

Jefferson Davis, the fifth son, was born April 4th, 1861. He married Miss Lizzie J. Smith, the daughter of James and Sally F. Smith, of Messongo, Va. They have one son, Royal D. Byrd, who was born March 31st, 1882. He was married to Miss Norcice L. Bloxom, the daughter of Martin and Susan J. Bloxom, on the 22d day of December, 1902. He is a prosperous farmer and lives near Mears P. O. in Accomack county, Va.

Levin J., the sixth son, was born December 26th, 1864. He lives in Baltimore and is doing business there.

Major Jackson Byrd, the seventh and youngest son of Parker and Mary A. Byrd (nee Trader), was born August 31st, 1867. He is unmarried and inherited his father's homestead, where he cared for him and ministered to his wants in his last days. Noble son he was.

Samuel C., the third son and survivor of twins of Johannas and Elana Byrd, was born October 30th, 1822. He grew up under

Christian influence and was noted for piety in early life. He was a bachelor and very religious, being quite eccentric. He made almost a thorough acquaintance with the Bible; he could quote the most of it from memory and tell nearly all the names and places mentioned therein. He told me, when on a visit to me once, that he had read his Bible through three times on his knees. While in conversation with him I said to him that he had been faithful in the service of his Lord for a long time, and now in advanced years I thought it would be better for him to select a good woman, suitable to his life and circumstances, and marry and be more retired, since he had traveled a long time and done all the good he could. To which he replied: "Oh, no; if I had a wife I would not have time to read my Bible." He was pious from his youth, and died March 15th, 1895, in the faith with a bright hope of his future reward.

William T. Byrd, fourth son of Johannas

and Elana Byrd, was born May 29th, 1824. He was a carpenter and followed that occupation for several years. On February 24th, 1853, he married Miss Hetty Ann Fisher. Afterwards he devoted most of his time to farming for the rest of his life, and was moderately successful. The fruit of their marriage was nine children. First, a daughter, Elizabeth H., born December 11th, 1853. She married Alfred S. Miles (date of marriage unknown) and died January 11th, 1885, leaving three children. Their names not known.

Georgeanna, the second daughter, was born August 14th, 1855, and died unmarried January 14th, 1885.

Tabitha S., third daughter, was born October 4th, 1857. She married William Hall (date of marriage not known). They live near Temperanceville, Accomack county, Va.

Cornelius J. Byrd, the fourth child and oldest son of William T. and Hetty Ann Byrd (nee Fisher), was born March 3d, 1860. He grew up on the farm with his parents.

He received a meagre education and adapted his life to farming with fair success, and was married to Rebecca J. Duncan, December 26th, 1883. They have issue. Bertha L., first daughter, born October 14th, 1884. She married Mr. Bates Pilchard, a worthy young farmer of Worcester county, Maryland, on the 22d day of February, 1905. Georgia A., second daughter, was born February 23d, 1889. She received her education at the High School in Pocomoke City, and was graduated there in 1906.

Othelia May, third daughter, was born February 4th, 1891. Ora Pearl, fourth and youngest daughter of Cornelius J. and Rebecca J. (Duncan) Byrd, was born August 31st, 1899.

Cornelius J. Byrd and wife, Rebecca, are natives of Accomack county, Virginia, but now reside in Worcester county, Maryland.

Hubbard Lee, fifth child of William T. Byrd and Hetty Ann, his wife, was born

June 15th, 1863. He married in Baltimore and is doing business there.

Martha F., the sixth child and youngest daughter, was born July 15th, 1865. She was married to Edward E. Nock, a worthy young man of Accomack county, Virginia, February 16th, 1888. Mr. Nock, at the time of his marriage, was engaged in a mercantile business as a traveling salesman, but later he took to farming and devotes his entire time to that occupation, residing now near Stockton, Md. He and his good wife have, as the result of their union, seven children. First, Harold E., born April 26th, 1889; second, Hattie F., born October 14th, 1890; third, Beulah M., born August 9th, 1894; fourth, William B., born November 22d, 1896; fifth, Margie, was born April 30th, 1898; sixth, Randolph M., born July 4th, 1902; Alton E., the seventh and youngest child of Edward E. and Martha F. (Byrd) Nock, was born April 19th, 1904. Mr. and

Mrs. Nock are both devoted and consistent members of the Baptist Church.

Arthur W. Byrd, seventh child of William T. and Hetty A. Byrd, was born December 23d, 1867. He was married to Rebecca Hall, the daughter of Thomas and Hester Hall, December 27th, 1893. As a result of their union they have only one child, a son, Colwell Francis Byrd, born May 3d, 1906, named for the writer of this work. They live at Oak Hall, Va.

Charles T., the eighth child, was born August 22d, 1869. He is a farmer and lives about one mile from Pocomoke City, in Worcester county, Md. He married Miss Mary Lambertson, December 27th, 1899. They have issue: Edith, first child, born November 19th, 1900, and Essie, second child, born August 31st, 1902.

Alonzo D. Byrd, ninth and youngest child of William T. and Hetty A. (Fisher) Byrd, was born June 19th, 1872. He married Martha F. Godwin, November 6th, 1895.

They have issue—Lena B., born January 12th, 1897; Edna S., born March 6th, 1898, and died December 8th, 1901; Lottie M., born July 20th, 1899; Walter H., born May 17th, 1901; Ernest M., born January 10th, 1903; Broadus F., born September 15th, 1904. He is a farmer and lives near Stockton, Md.

Elizabeth Custis Byrd, second daughter of Johannas Byrd and Elana Byrd (nee Cocke) was born October 26th, 1826. She was married to George Northam in June, 1859, and died childless in 1880.

Personal, Political and Religious.

I, Colwell Patterson Byrd, the seventh child and youngest son of Johannas Byrd and Elana (Cocke) Byrd, and the author of this work, was born in Accomack county, Virginia, on the 26th day of January, 1829. I grew up to manhood trained in the tenets of the old Whig party, feeling that it would almost be a dishonorable act for me to sup-

port any other party but the one which endured seven years warfare and bloodshed for American Liberty. In 1852, I cast my first vote for Winfield Scott, the Whig nominee for President of the United States of America.

But later on, as there become changes in the affairs of the nation, I changed my sentiments politically, and when the Rebellion took place in 1861 I voted with the Democratic party and have continued to do so ever since. As to my religious belief, I am a Baptist from principle and conviction. In early life I was impressed with the importance of my personal salvation, which impression has been lasting.

When about eighteen years of age, in 1847, I was apprenticed to a competent brick mason in Baltimore and acquired a knowledge of that useful trade.

I was religiously inclined from my childhood and received my first impression when about four years old, which impression has

remained with me nearly three score and fifteen years, although I did not make a public profession of religion until April, 1850; on the 5th day of that month I was baptized by the Rev. George F. Adams, in the Patapsco river at Canton, Baltimore, and was received into the fellowship of the Second Baptist Church of that city on the same day.

I still continued to live in Baltimore a few years, working at my trade, and on the 17th day of September, 1854, I married Elizabeth A. Trader, the daughter of William and Comphrate (Walker) Trader, of Accomack county, Virginia, a lady of a true Christian type. After our marriage we moved to Newtown, Worcester county, Md., now Pocomoke city, the 1st day of January, 1855. Three children were the result of our union.

Laura Grace Byrd, the first child and only daughter of Colwell P. and Elizabeth A. (Trader) Byrd, was born in Newtown, Wor-

cester county, Md., October 1st, 1855. She was educated at the High School of her birthplace, known now as the High School of Pocomoke City.

She was married to George W. Oldham, April 16th, 1874, a worthy young man of Temperanceville, Va., in the Newtown Baptist Church, now First Baptist Church of Pocomoke City, Md., by Rev. Montcalm Oldham, father of the bridegroom, assisted by Rev. Lemuel D. Paulding, pastor of the bride.

Mr. Oldham, when quite a young man, enlisted as a volunteer in the Confederate Army in April, 1863, and served until the close of the war, under Brigadier General Crutchfield, Division Commander Gen. W. H. F. Lee, and corps Commander General Ewell, called "Old Fox." He was also in Company E, 19th Virginia Battalion, Artillery, Capt. G. G. Savage commanding, Colonel Atkinson commanding battalion.

After the close of the war he remained for a few years in Richmond, Va., and then re-

turned to the Eastern Shore of Virginia and engaged in a mercantile business at Temperanceville, Accomack county, which business he was pursuing at the time of his marriage with Miss Byrd.

The result of their union was three children—Leroy Oldham, first child and only son of George W. and Laura Grace (Byrd) Oldham, was born in Temperanceville, Accomack county, Virginia, March 12th, 1875. He obtained a good business education and when quite young he was employed as clerk in the retail drug business in the city of Norfolk, Va., and remained there a short time, when he moved to Baltimore with his employer, and on the 20th of June, 1892, he accepted a position as clerk with Gilpin, Langdon & Co., one of the largest wholesale drug establishments in that city. Having push and vim with his capacity for business and commendable deportment of life, he found favor with his employers. Step by step he advanced in business until at the age of

Leroy Oldham,
Baltimore, Md.

thirty-two years he is now a prosperous wholesale druggist in the city of Baltimore.

He was married to Miss Mabel Ray Sharretts, daughter of Grayson W. and Maude Anna Sharretts, of Baltimore, in the Brown Memorial Presbyterian Church of that city, by Rev. Byron Clarke, of Mt. Washington, and Rev. John Timothy Stone, pastor of the bride, and is at the present time well situated at his home on Clifton Avenue, Walbrook, a suburb of Baltimore.

Since the writer closed this paragraph of the genealogy of this work, another event has taken place in the birth of his great granddaughter, Dorothy Byrd Oldham, the daughter of Leroy and Mabel Ray Oldham, born at 2800 Clifton Avenue, Walbrook, Baltimore, Md., October 26th, 1907; being the first born of his fourth generation whom he had the pleasure of holding in his arms and pronouncing a benediction upon the day after her birth.

Annie B., second child of George W. and

Laura Grace Oldham, was born December 2d, 1880, died September 3d, 1881.

Elizabeth Grace, the youngest daughter of George W. and Laura Grace Oldham (nee Byrd), was born March 4th, 1883. She was educated in the High School at Pocomoke city, Worcester county, and St. Michael's, Talbot county, Md. She is a lady of culture, and has prepared herself for teaching and is a teacher in the High School at Temperanceville, Va.

Franklin W. Byrd, only son and survivor of twins of Colwell P. and Elizabeth A. (Trader) Byrd, was born in Newtown, Worcester county, Md., July 20th, 1859. He was educated in the High School of his birthplace, now Pocomoke city. Very early in life, when a boy, his mind was turned toward mercantile pursuits. In youth he engaged in that business with a vim that characterizes men of energy and push. For a few years he was employed as clerk in a general merchandise business; later he was employed as

FRANKLIN W. BYRD,
POCOMOKE CITY, MD.

traveling salesman with a wholesale grocery house in Baltimore for several years. In June, 1895, he accepted a position with a large wholesale tobacco house, which position he still hólds. He is a stockholder and also one of the directors of the Citizens National Bank of Pocomoke city.

On February 20th, 1888, he was married to Miss Elizabeth P. Johnson, the daughter of Captain Hiram and Eliza Sebastian Johnson, of Westmoreland county, Virginia, in the Episcopal Church at Stockton, Md., by the rector, Rev. Mr. Batte, the pastor of the bride.

Two interesting daughters are the result of their union—Hallie Johnson Byrd, first child, ~~[illegible]~~. She was educated in her home school and graduated there ~~[illegible]~~ with great credit to herself. She is an interesting and accomplished young lady, and has quite a talent for music and will take a special course in that line of education.

Elizabeth Franklin, a bright and interesting four-year-old girl, the second and youngest daughter of Franklin W. and Elizabeth P. (Johnson) Byrd, ~~was born the fourth day of November, 1895.~~ She is a child of promise.

Colwell P. Byrd's first wife, Elizabeth A. (Trader) Byrd, was born October 10th, 1823, married September 17th, 1854, died March 20th, 1885. He married his present wife, Mary A. E. Parsons, of Seaford, Del., September 17th, 1890.

OBITUARY.

Words are inadequate to express the virtues of so lovely a woman. Rich in love, benevolence, good will, chaste in word, thought and deed; without envy, hatred, or vanity, she won the love and admiration of all who knew her. Twenty-two years have passed away since she died, but the roses that she propagated in her life and transplanted by her husband are still blooming on her grave.

The place will soon be forgotten, but she will live and adorn the race as long as there are any to remember and imitate her virtues. The following is her obituary written by her pastor:

Mrs. Elizabeth A. Byrd—This excellent lady, wife of Colwell P. Byrd, departed this life on Friday morning, March the 20th, 1885, at 2 o'clock, about sixty-one years of age. She had been sick some ten days or more, but had not been regarded as seriously ill until the day before her death. Her trouble seems to have been of a kidney character which of late has become so common. The death of this estimable woman has thrown another dark shadow over this community over which so many have recently passed in close succession; has sorely stricken another church, yet smarting from a recent stroke; has made another home, in which domestic bliss, wifely devotion, motherly tenderness, and the graces of true friend-

ship and sincere piety so long quietly reigned, lonely, dreary and desolate.

Mrs. Byrd was long a resident of Pocomoke City and was widely known in our community. She was highly esteemed for her noble personal qualities, her kindliness of heart, her gentleness of disposition, her readiness to befriend, to help to do good to others. Few, perhaps, had more or sincerer friends. She has been for years connected with the Baptist Church here. Though not one of its original members, she and her husband, for years one of its worthy deacons, early settled here after its organization and at once identified themselves with it. From its infancy to the day of her death was she connected with its history. And how worthy did she prove herself; how faithful and devoted to all its interests; how ready to engage in every good work. How she will be missed; how the church will miss her; how the Ladies' Society in their enterprises will miss her; how that stricken husband and

Mrs. Elizabeth A. Byrd (Mother),
Pocomoke City, Md.

those devoted children will miss her. But her work was done and the Master said "Come up higher." Her funeral services were held on Sunday afternoon in the Baptist Church, and though a violent snow storm was prevailing at the time, a large congregation of sympathizing friends was present. Her remains now sleep quietly in the Baptist Cemetery, but she has gone to live with Christ. We will not weep as those who have no hope.

SOLOMON CHARLES BOSTON.

Rachel Ann, third daughter and eighth child of Johannas and Elana Byrd (nee Cocke), was born August 8th, 1830. She grew up to be an interesting young lady, always carrying sunshine with her cheerful disposition, that characterized her short life. She was a model of beauty. I don't think Accomack county, Virginia, ever produced a prettier face on a woman than the one she wore. She was admired by both sexes of those who knew her.

In June, 1848, she was married to Thomas H. Fisher, an industrious young farmer at Messongo, Accomack county, Va. She died of diphtheria about the 29th of November, 1851, and left one child, Martin D. Fisher, who was born at Messongo, June 22d, 1849.

Mr. Fisher remained in his native county a few years after the death of his wife. In 1855 he went to New Orleans and remained there until the fall of that year. From there he visited Audrain county, Missouri. In 1856 he returned to the Eastern Shore of Virginia. After a short stay near his old home, he took his son, Martin D., a seven year old boy, and returned to Audrain county, Missouri, and settled near the town of Mexico in that county, and remained there until his death, the date of which I have no record. His son, Martin D. Fisher, grew up and was educated in Audrain county, Missouri, and in the twenty-fourth year of his age he was married to Miss Jane D. Wilson March 11th, 1873, in Audrain county, Mis-

souri. To them have been born four sons: First, Byrd Fisher, born in Audrain county, Missouri, December 22, 1873, died April 19th, 1879; Francis Selby, the second son, born also in Audrain county, Missouri, November 24th, 1876. After the birth of their second son, Mr. and Mrs. Fisher visited the Eastern Shore of Virginia, I think sometime in 1877. After reaching his place of nativity Mr. Fisher decided to remain, and taught school several years, during which time their third son, Ira Sidney Fisher, was born, in Accomack county, Virginia, on the 19th day of April, 1889. Soon after birth of their third son, they concluded to go back to Missouri again about the latter part of 1881. And on the 22d of April, 1885, Willie Clay Fisher, fourth and youngest son of Martin D. and Jane D. Fisher (nee Wilson) was born in Audrain county, Missouri, and died there in infancy.

In the month of March, 1893, Mr. and Mrs. Fisher returned with their two sons, Francis

Selby and Ira Sidney, to Accomack county, Virginia, located at Hallwood Station, and continued there until 1905, when they moved to Jamaica, N. Y., where they now reside.

Francis Selby Fisher, oldest son of Martin D. and Jane D. Fisher, was married to Miss Lillie Bertha Gray, in Accomack county, Virginia, October 25th, 1898. They have issue— only daughter, Nellie Gray Fisher, born in Accomack county, Virginia, on the 31st day of March, 1900. They reside now in New York city.

Ira Sidney, the youngest son, was married to Miss Umstaddt March 28th, 1905, in Mexico, Audrain county, Missouri, where they now reside.

Mr. and Mrs. Fisher are both consistent members of the Old School Baptist Church. He and his two sons are descendants of the Byrd family on the mother's side. They are all carpenters by trade.

Mary F. Byrd, the youngest child of Johannes and Elana (Cocke) Byrd, was born

JOHANNAS L. BYRD
OAK HALL, VA.

June 12th, 1833. She was married to Littleton T. Byrd, her cousin, in 1852. Three children were the result of their union—First, Olivia, born January, 1853, and died in infancy; the second child (not named) also died in infancy; Johannas L. Byrd, third child and only son of Littleton T. and Mary F. Byrd, was born January 7th, 1855. He married Miss Elizabeth E. Parks, December 20th, 1876, the daughter of John and Katie Parks, of Messongo, Accomack county, Va. They have issue—Lillie Francis, first child, born September 28th, 1877; second, Mary Susan, born February 6th, 1880. She was married to Mr. Oswald S. Mears November 4th, 1896. He is employed as agent for the N. Y. P. & N. R. R. Co., and resides at Bloomtown, Virginia. They have issue, two children—first child, born November 21st, 1899, and died August 1st, 1900; second child, Lee Kerns, born May 31st, 1902.

Third child of Johannas L. and Elizabeth (Parks) Byrd, Otho Littleton, was born Feb-

ruary 15th, 1883; fourth, Orris Sylvester, born June 23, 1886; the fifth, James Milton, was born October 28th, 1888; sixth, Nannie Eliza, born January 17th, 1893; seventh, Walter Rhodes, was born November 23d, 1898.

Mr. Byrd is employed by the N. Y. P. & N. R. R. Co. He and his wife reside at Oak Hall, Accomack county, Va.

I am indebted to my nephew, Major Jackson Byrd, for a verbatim copy of his grandfather's will, bearing date of September 23d, 1853, which is as follows:

"In the name of God, Amen. I, Johannas Byrd, being of sound and perfect memory (blessed be God) and being convinced of the uncertainty of life and the necessity of a preparation for death, do hereby make this my last will in manner and form following, and do revoke any and other wills heretofore made by me. First and principally: I commend my soul to God that gave it and my body to be buried in such decent order as my

executors, hereafter named, shall think meet and convenient. And, as touching the disposition of my worldly estate as it hath pleased God in his mercy to bestow upon me.

Item First. I lend to my daughter Elizabeth the largest room in my dwelling house during her single life and also fire-wood for said room.

"Second. I give and bequeath to my son, Jacob K. Byrd, the land whereon I now live together with all the appurtenances thereto belonging and bounded by a straight ditch running from the county road easterly up to land of Henry Young's heirs; to him, the said Jacob K. Byrd, and his heirs forever.

"Third. I give and bequeath to my son, Parker Byrd, the place on which said Parker now lives, containing fifty acres, more or less, and bounded as follows; beginning at a marked white oak between the heirs of Henry Young, deceased, and said land running northwesterly so as to make his woodland

as wide where it joins the land of James Northam as it is where it joins the land of Henry Young's heirs, to him, the said Parker Byrd, and heirs forever.

"Fourth. I give and bequeath to my son, Samuel C. Byrd, residue or remainder of my land, it being forty-seven and one-half acres, more or less, to him and his heirs forever.

"Fifth. I give and bequeath to my daughter, Margaret, one bed and furniture, second choice, and the chest that was her mother's.

"Sixth. I also authorize my son Parker to hold in his possession my negro girl Sarah and a reasonable hire for whom I require said Parker to pay to my daughter Margaret, but neither said negro or her hire is to be subject to the control of said Margaret's husband or in any wise liable for his debts, and if said Margaret die before said Parker, in that event I give said negro, Sarah, to my said son Parker.

"Seventh. I give and bequeath my negro woman, Mary, and her increase if she have

any after this time, also a bed and furniture, the first choice, to my daughter Elizabeth.

"Eighth. I give and bequeath to my daughter, Polly, my negro, George, and bed and furniture, third choice.

"Ninth. I give and bequeath to my son, William T. Byrd, my negro boy, John, and the whole of my carpenter and joiner's tools.

"Tenth. I give and bequeath to my son, Colwell P. Byrd, his heirs or assigns, my negro boy, Robert.

Also, I leave the remainder of my personal property to be sold and, after paying my just debts, to be divided as follows: the one-fourth to my daughter Elizabeth, one-fourth to my daughter Polly, one-fourth to my grandchildren John, Eliza, Alexander, Washington, George and William Cutler. And also one-fourth to my grandson Martin Fisher.

"I hereby authorize my son, Jacob K. Byrd, to retain the amount designed for the

Cutler children and lay it out for their schooling, unless necessity should otherwise require it.

"If either of said Cutler children die before receiving his or her distributive share, I give the portion designed for him or her to the surviving ones.

"I require my sons Jacob, Parker and Samuel to bear an equal proportion in feeding and clothing my afflicted negro man, Elijah, and when he dies to have him decently buried.

"I appoint my sons, Jacob K. and Parker Byrd, my executors. In testimony whereof I hereunto set my hand this, the twenty-third day of September, in the year of our Lord, eighteen hundred and fifty-three.

"WITNESS: JOHANNAS BYRD. (Seal)."
MARTIN K. KELLY.
SYLVESTER J. MARSHALL.
JOHN H. CUSTIS.

Daniel T. Byrd, youngest son of Nathaniel and Naomi (Watson) Byrd, was born Octo-

ber 30th, 1785, and died at the old Byrd homestead at Muddy Creek, Accomack county, Va., on March 30th, 1846, where he had spent all his life. He grew up on the farm and devoted his entire life to that occupation. He was married to Nancy Gillespie about March, 1811. There were born to them two children—

Nathaniel J. Byrd, the first child and only son of Daniel T. and Nancy (Gillespie) Byrd, was born at the old homestead February 8th, 1812. He grew up and was educated in the ordinary school of his day, later he acquired a knowledge of the carpenter's trade and pursued that occupation for a few years in his native State, after which, in the early thirties, 1833 or 1834, he went to the State of Missouri with a colony of young men and women (mostly men). The company consisted of about thirty persons from Worcester county, Maryland, and Accomack county, Virginia. In that company there was a newly married couple, Mr. Asa

Merrill and his bride, who was Miss Ann Aydelotte Mason. They used that opportunity for their wedding tour. That company all sailed together on board of a schooner from Cedar Hall wharf, on the Pocomoke river, in Worcester county, Maryland, to Baltimore, as steamboats and railroads were something unknown in that country at that time. Arriving in Baltimore by sailboat, from thence they took their tedious and fatiguing journey to Missouri by stage.

When they reached their destination, they dispersed to different parts of the State. Mr. Merrill and his bride and Mr. Byrd settled in Lafayette county, near the town of Lexington, Missouri. Mr. Byrd pursued his chosen occupation, the carpenter's trade, and taught school at intervals—until the summer of 1835, at which time he returned to his native home in Accomack county, Virginia, on a visit to his father and other relatives, for a short period of time. Upon returning to Missouri, later in the same year,

he resumed his work at the carpenter's bench. In the meantime it pleased God in the allwise dispensation of His Providence to remove, by death, Mr. Merrill, from his new home and settlement in this life, to his destiny beyond, leaving his young widow and his orphan son, Levin H. Merrill. The date of his birth, the writer does not know, but probably it was some time in 1834, judging from some other incidents that occurred in that family of which I have been informed.

Mrs. Merrill remained a widow until about the Autumn of 1837, when at that time she again united in matrimony with Nathaniel J. Byrd, mentioned above. Her son, Levin H. Merrill, grew up to manhood and when the war between the States came on he went in the Confederate service and was killed in Arkansas, leaving a widow and several children. Mrs. Byrd was born in Worcester county, Maryland, November 28th, 1808. She was left an orphan at about eight years old

and was raised by her uncle, a Presbyterian preacher, who lived near Snow Hill.

She was first cousin to the late Col. William J. Aydelotte, of Pocomoke City, Md. She was a lady of worthy reputation and noble traits. I remember meeting Judge James Merrill (who was a native of Worcester county, Maryland, but had resided in Lafayette county, Missouri, for many years) in 1856 in Newtown, now Pocomoke City, while on a visit to friends and relatives in his native county, and, in answer to my inquiry for Nathaniel J. Byrd he told me that he was well acquainted with him and his family.

Mrs. Byrd, who was the widow of Asa Merrill, who was born in Worcester county, Maryland, (date of birth not known) and died in Lexington, Mo., about the year 1835, had, by her second marriage with Nathaniel J. Byrd, seven children, whose names are as follows:

Asa Nathaniel, first son of Nathaniel J.

and Ann Aydelotte Byrd, was born July 12th, 1838, at Lexington, Mo. He was educated in the country schools and in 1855 he became a member of the United Baptist Church. In 1860 he entered The William Jewell College at Liberty, Mo., as a student for the gospel ministry, from which place he received the degree A. B. and the degree A. M. He was ordained to the full work of the gospel ministry on the sixth day of March, 1864, by the Second Baptist Church of Liberty, Mo. The council was composed of William Thompson, president of William Jewell College, Edward J. Owen, professor of William Jewell College, Thomas H. Stouts, professor of William Jewell College, J. B. Tombes, president of Woman's College, W. C. Barrett, pastor, W. J. Patrick.

The Rev. Asa N. Byrd spent his life work in the gospel ministry within the bounds of the North Liberty Baptist Association, which was organized at New Hope Baptist Church, Clay county, Mo., in 1844, where he was

highly complimented at their jubilee celebration, held in 1894, by Dr. W. R. Rothwell, the principal speaker of that occasion, who said if he was called upon to name the minister who has been pastor of more churches, who had conducted more funeral services, and married more couples than any one minister in that Association, he would name the tenor-voiced Asa N. Byrd.

He was married June 21st, 1866, to Miss Sallie E. Pemberton, of near Platt city, Platt county, Mo., who (the writer has been informed) was a lady of high attainments and an efficient helpmeet to her husband in his ministerial work for nearly forty years. Her Heavenly Father took her from her work on earth to her reward in Heaven in the fall of 1904, leaving her bereaved husband (now a retired Baptist preacher, and living about one and a half miles from Liberty, Mo.), with his two noble and accomplished daughters, Mattie and Annie, to bless his home,

both of whom are graduates of the Woman's College of Liberty.

The second birth was that of William Daniel T. and twin sister, Mary Ann, born about 1840 (the exact date of birth unknown). William grew up to manhood. He was by profession a photographer. He married young and died childless.

Mary Ann, the twin sister, grew up to womanhood, married a Mr. Offut, and died childless. The third, Sarah Rebecca, who grew up to womanhood with brilliant intellect, was a teacher of promise and died unmarried in the twenty-second year of her age.

The fifth child, Demmeria, was born at Lexington, Mo., (date of birth not known). She grew up to womanhood and married John Barton, a farmer near Springfield, Mo. They have a family of several children and now reside in Arkansas.

Ayres M., the youngest son, who is a dealer in pianos and musical instruments, lives at 426 Topping avenue, Kansas City,

Mo. He has one son, Leslie, with whom the writer corresponded a few times several years ago.

Fannie, the youngest child of Nathaniel J. and Ann A. (Merrill) Byrd, (nee Mason), was born at Odessa, Mo., (the exact date of birth unknown, but is supposed to have been about 1848). She was educated in her home school in Odessa, and in early life was married to Mr. W. T. Thomason, a teacher. They remained in Missouri several years after their marriage, but subsequently moved to Fayetteville, Ark., with their two daughters, where they now reside. Their eldest daughter, Demma, died several years ago, unmarried. Annie, the youngest daughter, married a Mr. Dunlap (date of marriage unknown). He is a graduate of Effingham School of Photography, Illinois. They lived in Fayetteville after their marriage until July, 1907, when they moved to Clifton, Ariz. They have two children, who, with their

mother, are descendants of the Byrd family of Accomack county, Virginia.

Mr. and Mrs. Nathaniel J. Byrd both lived to a ripe old age. Mrs. Byrd was a consistent member of the Presbyterian Church for a number of years, but afterward became a Baptist, and at the age of sixty years she was enrolled as a charter member of Mt. Hope Baptist Church, now of Odessa, Mo., where she died on March 10th, 1885, at the age of seventy-five years. She preceded her husband in death about nineteen years. He died in Springfield, Mo., in January, 1904, at the advanced age of ninety-two years.

Demmeria, the only daughter of Daniel T. and Nancy Byrd (nee Gillespie), was born at the old Byrd homestead about August, 1813. She was married to George P. Byrd, a worthy young man and farmer, about the spring of 1836. They lived about half a mile from her birthplace. The result of their union was four children.

Betsy Poulson Byrd, their first child, was

born probably in the early part of 1838. She died in childhood. I cannot record the date of the births of the other three children. Decatur Franklin was the second child. He lived to middle age and died unmarried.

Osborne, the third child, lived nearby his birthplace until he arrived at manhood and then went to a dental school and studied that profession. Later on he went to Indian Territory, and practiced his profession. There he married a half-breed Indian lady, who is said to be a very fine woman, settled there, and had issue. I have met his two daughters, who visited Accomack county, Virginia, their father's native county.

Susan, the fourth child of George P. and Demmeria Byrd, is unmarried and lives with her brother in Indian Territory.

Daniel T. Byrd's children of his second marriage with Rhoda Riggin, in 1814, are as follows: Daniel T., Jr., first child, son of Daniel T. and Rhoda (Riggin) Byrd, was born at Muddy Creek, in the old Byrd home-

stead, February 17th, 1815. He grew up to manhood and learned the carpenter's trade. In 1839 he went to New York and pursued his chosen occupation for about ten years, during which time he married and settled in Williamsburg, then a suburban town of New York. During his stay in that locality his wife died and left him with three children, one of them I had the pleasure of meeting in 1846 at her grandfather's in Accomack county, Virginia, an interesting little girl of about six years. In 1848 he united again in matrimony with Miss Susan Fisher, of Accomack county, Virginia, and in the latter part of 1849 he moved to California with his family in search of gold, and soon after we lost all trace of him and family.

Samuel, the second son, was born about June, 1817. He married Mrs. Elizabeth Byrd (nee Taylor), in December, 1846. The result of their union was one child, Sally, the only daughter of Samuel and Elizabeth Byrd, who was born about the latter part of 1847 (the

exact date of birth unknown). Mr. Byrd was a farmer, devoted his life to that occupation and died in the fall of 1852.

Obed S. Byrd, the third son of Daniel T. and Rhoda Byrd, was born September 12th, 1819, and died at the old homestead place August 25th, 1876. He was a farmer and pursued that calling all his life. He married Miss Hetty Mears in 1853, the daughter of Thomas and Katie Mears, of Guilford, Accomack county, Va. They had issue.

Florence Neil, the oldest child (daughter) on the family record of Obed S. and Hetty (Mears) Byrd, was born February 11th, 1857.

Daniel Harmanson, the second child (son) was born October 8th, 1859. Rhoda Ann C., the third child, was born February 8th, 1862. She was married to James T. Smith, May 31st, 1882. They reside on the homestead place at Muddy Creek, Va. Warren L., the fourth child, was born November 7th, 1864. Thomas Woodson, the fifth and youngest

child of Obed S. and Hetty (Mears) Byrd, was born March 21st, 1875. The children of Obed S. Byrd all live near the place of their birth.

Littleton T., the fourth child of Daniel T. and Rhoda Byrd, was born April 22d, 1821, and died in 1855. He left a widow and one child. Emeline, the oldest daughter of Daniel T. and Rhoda Byrd, was born March the 16th, 1823, and died unmarried about the year 1860.

Eliza, the youngest daughter, was born March 9th, 1826. She married Alfred Riggin, her cousin, in 1852, and died childless in October, 1854.

Riley Franklin Byrd, the youngest child of Daniel T. and Rhoda Byrd (nee Riggin) was born February 10th, 1830. He was educated in the best schools in Accomack county, Virginia. He studied surveying and navigation, acquired a knowledge of these two studies and later on studied medicine, but never practiced it. He was of a roving disposi-

tion, and having no fixed purpose he took to the sea and followed that course of life for a while. He then abandoned that pursuit, began teaching for a livelihood, and taught school all along the Atlantic States, from Georgia to Nova Scotia, and late in his life he returned to his native State and taught until the time of his death in December, 1904, and was buried in the old family graveyard with his parents at Muddy Creek, Accomack county, Va.

The author of the preceding genealogy feels painfully aware that he has come far from compiling a perfect history of this branch of the worthy family of whom he has endeavored to make a record, and having, as aforesaid, made diligent research among the archives at the county seat of Accomack county, Virginia, and not being able to find any records that give satisfactory information of the exact time of settlement in the locality named, we find it necessary to follow tradition, which has already been quoted.

Furthermore, there is a tradition which says that two men named Byrd came to the Eastern Shore in the early part of 1700 from the Western Shore of Virginia (the exact place whence they came is not known to the writer) and found their way up the Pocomoke Sound. One of these men, whose name was Nathaniel Byrd, located on Muddy Creek, in Accomack county, Va., about that time. The other man, of whose first name we are not positive, settled in the southern part of Somerset county, Maryland, near the place where the town of Crisfield is now built. By recent search in the clerk's office at Princess Anne, Somerset county, Md., I find that the records of deeds and wills at that place show that David Byrd willed property in that county to his daughter, Eliza Byrd, in 1722, which corresponds quite authentically to the time of the settlement of that branch of the Byrd family which settled at Muddy Creek, Accomack county, Va.

Also the records at the same place show

that Joseph Byrd deeded legacies to his wife, Arabella Byrd, on the first day of August, 1739. I also find that the same records at Princess Anne show that Arabella Byrd willed property in Somerset county, Maryland, on July 19th, 1745.

The will of Thomas Byrd, on record and registered among the wills and deeds at Princess Anne, Somerset county, Md., bearing date 1747, show that he willed his property, to be equally divided among his six children, viz: Elizabeth Sterling, Hannah Wilson, Jacob Byrd, Rachel Byrd, Betsy Byrd and Polly Byrd. The above dates correspond very closely to the traditional accounts of the Byrd family of Muddy Creek, Va., and the names mentioned here bear a very close resemblance to some of the names of that branch of the family and almost conclusively verify the authenticity of their record.

There were other Byrds who settled in the locality of Muddy Creek subsequently to the

time of the first settlers, of whom the writer has made no record. They may have been slightly relatd, but it is only of his own immediate ancestry that the author has written. And just here he will mention some of their customs and manners of life. They were of English origin, and doubtless they and the generations which have followed them have all come down in a line of descent from Col. William Byrd, who came from England in 1670, and settled at Westover, on the James river, in Virginia.

I will now use this space in which to relate an incident that occurred in the life of Colonel Byrd, which has been furnished me by a lady who is a native of Virginia. On one occasion he was on a visit to Governor Spotswood, of Virginia, and, among the other pets which the Governor had at home, was a beautiful fawn. While the company was seated at the dinner table, at which Colonel Byrd was the guest of honor, the fawn came up and, looking through an open window,

saw reflected in the large mirror, hanging on the opposite wall, its picture. Thinking it another deer, the fawn made a dart through the window and crashed into the mirror, also the china from which the dinner was being served, making quite a scene and one long to be remembered by those present. Surely it was quite a memorable visit for Colonel Byrd to the Governor of Virginia.

The following is an extract taken from an article by Alice Broaddus Mitchell in "Kind Words," published in Nashville, Tenn.:

"It has been said that the primitive Virginians were not such readers as the Puritans, but there is sufficient reason to believe from what has been learned of the prominent men of Colonial times that they were highly cultured in those days. And in what we gather from this we find a very noticeable feature in the character and life of Colonel Byrd. So far as we have been able to learn of him he must have cherished a great fondness for culture and literature, from the fact

WILLIAM BYRD NORTHAM, JR., ESQ.,
CHESTER, PA.

that he had in his home at Westover a solid library that numbered nearly 4,000 volumes."

And still there remains to this time high aspirations in the minds of many of the descendants of that worthy name, that move them in the pursuit of culture and useful callings in life. The writer has in mind some of the offspring of that family of Byrds of Muddy Creek, Accomack county, Va., of whom he has endeavored to give a brief account.

The following are a few of the names which are worthy of mention: Hon. John R. Rew and his brother, I. Harry Rew. They are both prominent lawyers and practice in the courts of Accomack. Their mother was Cynthia E. Byrd, born at Muddy Creek, in the homestead of her grandfather, Parker Byrd. They are the fourth generation of said Parker Byrd of 1769, on the mother's side of the family. Also William Byrd Northam, Jr., of Chester, Pa., who is a young lawyer of promise and practices his

profession in that city. His grandmother was Margaret Byrd, and his maternal great-grandfather was Johannas Byrd, of 1777, in Accomack county, Virginia. The Rev. Asa N. Byrd, an eminent Baptist minister of Liberty, Clay county, Mo. He is of the third generation from Daniel T. Byrd, of 1785, at the old Byrd homestead of Muddy Creek, Va. These men, having a purpose in view to elevate their fellow man socially and religiously, with many other of their kindred, who are pursuing honorable vocations in the business world, are of this branch of the Byrd family of Muddy Creek, Va.

The writer has learned from parental and ancestral information that this branch of the Byrd family was a sturdy and valorous people, quite domestic in their habits, of upright integrity, true in their principles and of honest dealings. They were not wealthy, neither were any of them poor. They lived on their own resources, had plentiful supplies for all their demands and met their ob-

Rev. Asa N. Byrd
Liberty, Mo

ligations faithfully. They were mostly farmers and lived on their own farms. They were not selfish people but were always ready to show kindness to each other in doing neighborly favors in alternate turns. Their social life was of the most friendly manner.

Well does the writer call to memory the good old days, as far back as three score and ten years, how their social life at that time corresponded with the information that he had of their primitive customs as they would gather at his father's house for an evening's pleasure. The company would be seated in semi-circle around the spacious room before a large open fire-place, with a blazing fire in view. The women would be picking the seeds from the cotton, knitting or doing some other needed work, preparatory to the making of useful apparel, and enjoy talking about their geese, turkeys and other household affairs, while the men would be engaged in speaking of their ordinary interests or discussing some political matter concerning the

great Henry Clay or Daniel Webster or of some other worthy statesman, until a proper leaving time, and after participating in eating apples or sweet potatoes roasted by the big fire, before which they had spent the evening, and enjoying a glass of sweet cider they would bid adieu and go to their homes, all feeling that they had spent a delightful evening. Such were the pleasant times in which our ancestors lived.

I do not know that they entertained any political sentiment in their former days except that they regarded themselves subject to the English crown, until the war, declared by the thirteen United Colonies against Great Britian for their national liberty—The Revolutionary War. Then, as I have been informed, they co-operated with their own loved America in assisting to obtain their freedom from a tyrannical government. There were no Tories among them. They all adopted the true Whig principles, were loyal citizens of their loved country, and their

political sentiments ran down with the old line Whig party until it became extinct about the year 1854, when it was abandoned.

Their mode of religious worship, as I have learned, was of the Established Church of England until about the latter part of the 18th century, and as the churches in those days were so sparsely located, the worshipers very probably rendered much of their devotional service to Almighty God at their homes. I have seen my good old grandmother's prayer book, read prayers from it in my boyhood days and found therein contained some of the most excellent devotional sentiment. I have also in my possession at this time a volume of the Rev. Mr. Yorik's sermons, a very old book, printed in the old fashion type which is quite difficult for young readers of these days to understand. I am quite sure that my grandmother read these sermons from that old book when it was not convenient for her to attend the public worship.

It was soon after the beginning of the Revolutionary War that this Byrd family began to change their former religious views. On the fourth day of July, 1776, as I have been informed, a Baptist minister, by the name of Elijah Baker, came from the Western Shore of Virginia and located near the head of Old Plantation Creek, in Northampton county, Eastern Shore, Va., and preached the Gospel there, instructing the people in Baptist views as he had received them from the New Testament, and continued to preach all along this peninsula from the Capes of Virginia as far as Salisbury, which at that time was in Worcester county, Maryland, now Wicomico county, founded several churches along the lower part of the Peninsula and suffered bitter persecution for promulgating his religious views. He was fined and imprisoned in the county jail at Drummond Town, in Accomack county, Va., the same old historic jail that was built several hundred years ago, still remains there

to this day and is yet used for a prison. The writer visited this old romantic building in January, 1907, and found it a very ancient and gloomy looking place. It was there that this man of God was punished and forbidden to preach the Gospel under heavy penalty, which was placed upon him, and other severe trials that he endured, but like the old servant of God, he did not let any of these things move him, not being daunted by the hindrances that he found in his way, he boldly and faithfully preached the gospel wherever he could get hearers.

I have been informed that during the summer of 1777 he preached in a grove near the head of Muddy Creek in Accomack county, Va., held religious meetings there and baptized a number of converts, among whom was Naomi Byrd, the writer's grandmother, in that stream of water, and which is still used for the administration of that ordinance and where now stands a large and influential

Baptist church. From about that time the Byrd family of Muddy Creek accepted the Baptist views of Christianity and many of them still hold on to their faith, though many of their descendants have accepted the views of the Methodist, of both branches of that church, and worship with those denominations, while some of them may belong to other Protestant denominations. I never knew but one Catholic in this branch of the Byrd family.

Much more might be said of this worthy family, but from the jottings we have obtained we learn that, though there may be retrogrades, as is the case in almost all families, we notice that they were among the noted worthies that graced the soil of Virginia, and many of their numerous descendants are now living in quite a number of the States of the Union.

Since the author of this work began his effort (January, 1907) to produce this brief

genealogy and history, he has received many kind words of approval and appreciation from members of the family in different parts of the country, also many expressions of desire that the issue might be a success, coupled with a desire to obtain a copy of the book. But from the fact that only the Byrd family is expected to be interested in its history, my receipts may fall short of the outlay in money for its publication, aside from the large amount of time and labor expended on it. For this I have no regrets, for it has been a labor of love on my part and it is an inexpressible satisfaction to me that I have dug up from obscurity, as it were, and put in desirable form, a history of the family, that can be perused by the present generation and handed down to those who follow after us. I trust it has tended to draw the family much nearer together and has aroused an increased interest in family history and genealogy that will influence the

family, in future, to keep better records, etc., in all of which I feel that I have my reward.

COLWELL P. BYRD.

Pocomoke City, Md., January, 1908.

2760 1